Five Keys

to

Health and Healing

Hope for Body, Mind, and Spirit

GREGORY L. JANTZ, PHD
WITH KEITH WALL

Contents

Introduction: Hope Begins Here......................5

Key #1 Harness Your Thoughts........................... 9

Key #2 Heal Your Emotions..............................29

Key #3 Nurture Your Relationships 49

Key #4 Nourish Your Body..................................69

Key #5 Deepen Your Spirit 93

Notes.. 110

Hope Begins Here

Chances are there is an obstacle in your life you desperately want to overcome. You are seeking health and healing for something that is weighing you down or holding you back.

There's a good chance, too, that you are courageous and tenacious, because you are choosing to take the first steps on your path toward wholeness and well-being.

Everyone struggles with challenges, ailments, distress, or heartache of some kind. As a psychologist, I hear the details of people's troubles each week. These people tell me things like . . .

- "I feel so depressed. I can hardly get out of bed in the morning."

- "My marriage is falling apart, and honestly, I'm responsible for many of our problems."

- "I started taking painkillers and now they've taken over my life."

- "My teenage daughter walked out of the house, insisting she'd never be back. I am heartbroken and terrified for her."

- "When my son died, I felt like I died, too. In fact, a big part of me really did die."

Your individual situation might sound different from these, but you probably resonate with the sense of anguish conveyed by these words. To some degree, we've all been there. We've all broken down in times of weakness. We've all suffered difficulties, brought

pain on ourselves, denied our problems, and endured heartbreak inflicted by life's tragedies or the unkind acts of others.

A Foundation *for* Hope

If you and I had the opportunity to sit down and talk together, you would notice that the word *hope* comes up again and again. That's because I am a resolutely hopeful person, and I want everyone to be sustained and strengthened by the same foundation of hope.

Hopefulness is not wishful thinking, unfounded optimism, or pie-in-the-sky idealism. It is a choice we make to believe in our own capacity to overcome any challenge and, more so, to believe in a loving God who watches over us and always wants the best for us.

HOPEFULNESS IS A CHOICE WE MAKE TO BELIEVE IN OUR OWN CAPACITY TO OVERCOME ANY CHALLENGE.

I appreciate the words of the Old Testament proverb: "Hope deferred makes the heart sick, but a longing fulfilled is a tree of life" (Proverbs 13:12). This is more than a pithy phrase found on a poster or kitchen plaque. This is ancient wisdom that is applicable to our present day. A lack of hope only adds to a person's woes, but a heart full of hope leads to life.

That is the spirit in which I present the insights for health and healing in the pages ahead. I want these proven and practical strategies to serve as a springboard for you to experience joy and wholeness in your life.

Harness *Your* Thoughts

If you've been living on planet earth for any length of time, you know many things are out of your control. The economy. The weather. Job layoffs. What other people say, think, or how they behave. Not to mention a plethora of other circumstances that impact your life every day.

Most of us spend an inordinate amount of time worrying about things we *can't* influence without taking charge of the things we *can* influence. Our thoughts fall into this category.

Jack Canfield, leadership expert and *Chicken Soup for the Soul* coauthor, says, "You only have control over three things in your life: the thoughts you think, the images you visualize, and the actions you take."

Why is it so important to take charge of your thoughts? As said by minister Chuck Swindoll, "Thoughts, positive or negative, grow stronger with repetition."

If those quotes aren't enough to convince you of the influence our thought-lives have on health and healing, you may be interested to know what researchers at the Mayo Clinic say on the subject. According to experts at the renowned academic medical center, our thoughts impact our life span, rates of depression, levels of distress, psychological and physical well-being, heart health, risk of death from heart disease, how we cope with stress, how often we come down with the common cold, and much more.[1]

If you want to live your best life and master the keys to health and healing, the place to start is by harnessing your thoughts.

Healing Begins *in* Your Head

Over the course of three decades, I have counseled scores of people struggling with many different types of problems. Each of these painful situations has confirmed a truth I learned years ago: *What goes on in your head will come out in your actions, attitudes, and ambitions.*

WHAT GOES ON IN YOUR HEAD WILL COME OUT IN YOUR ACTIONS, ATTITUDES, AND AMBITIONS.

Your thoughts—the messages you speak or think to yourself every day—profoundly and powerfully determine every aspect of your life. What you tell yourself *about* yourself can radically influence your happiness, your relationships, and your physical well-being.

This presents a good news / bad news scenario. If your thoughts are consistently affirming, optimistic, and constructive, your life is sure to advance in a positive direction. But if your thoughts are consistently critical, pessimistic, and destructive, your life will advance in a negative direction.

I'm sure you like the sound of a *positive* rather than *negative* direction. So begin paying close attention to your self-talk and those silent-but-powerful internal messages you continually send yourself. As psychologist Les Parrott explained:

> Most of the time we have little awareness of our internal dialogue. Yet this self-talk has a huge impact on how you feel about yourself. It is the single most important determiner of whether or not you feel profound significance at your core. Your self-talk is a primary tool for realizing your lovability. . . . Healthy persons are keenly aware of what they say to themselves, how they say it, and when they say it.[2]

Your internal voice is the most powerful and influential voice in your life.

Your Thoughts Steer Your Direction

Imagine this scenario. You've always dreamed of sailing to the Hawaiian Islands. The golden shores, the swaying palm trees, the turquoise sea . . . paradise awaits.

So, you arrange to set out in a sailboat from San Diego. You provision your craft with everything for an enjoyable voyage—food, beverages, music, fishing gear. You also attend to all the safety precautions, including life jackets, emergency flares, and a radio transmitter.

You check and double-check the map, coordinates, and navigation system. You're good to go.

What you *don't* realize, however, is that your navigation system is malfunctioning ever so slightly—it's misaligned by just .005 degrees. As the miles pass—fifty, then a hundred, then a thousand—your boat veers off course without you knowing it. In fact, you bypass Hawaii completely and end up in the middle of the vast ocean.

The point of this scenario is that our lives follow a certain trajectory. The slightest shift in thought has the power to alter things dramatically . . . either for ill or for good. Why not make it for good?

We live in a culture enamored with the instant solution and the extreme makeover. *But when it comes to lasting personal and professional growth, change is most often steady and gradual.* If we want true transformation, we must readjust the navigation system in our brain.

Many people tell me they're stuck in a dead-end job, anxious about their children, struggling to kick a bad habit, or worried about finances.

IF WE WANT TRUE TRANSFORMATION, WE MUST READJUST THE NAVIGATION SYSTEM IN OUR BRAIN.

Though I don't dismiss the reality of these problems, most of the difficulties we wrestle with are *internal* rather than *external*. What goes on in our mind, heart, and soul largely determines where we'll eventually "arrive" with any issue we face.

Let's say the typical person has five hundred thousand thoughts each day. And let's say half of those are negative: "This job stinks . . . This outfit makes me look fat . . . My life is amounting to nothing." If that individual could turn .005 of those thoughts from negative to positive, incredible changes would occur. As time went on, that course correction would pay off in a big way.

Think of one aspect of your life in which you're concerned about the direction you're heading. It might be career, marriage, parenting, friendships, education, or physical fitness. Now consider how a .005 change in attitude and actions might alter your course . . . and ultimately, your destination.

Course Correction

Old ways of thinking often put up a fierce fight when challenged by something new. But you are not a mere bystander witnessing a boxing match between good thoughts and bad thoughts. It's within your power to choose which ideas you feed and which you starve. Nurture the helpful, healing thoughts while banishing the ones that bring you down and cause you doubt.

What difference would it make if your self-talk were affirmative and hopeful, with messages like these?

- I respect myself and deserve to be respected.

- God has created me just the way I am—and I'm so glad he did.

- I have plenty of shortcomings but am becoming the person I was fully meant to be.

- I feel good about the way I look, and I don't need to compare myself with anyone.

■ I am valuable and worthy of love just the way I am.

When you use self-talk like this, a new world of self-acceptance begins to unfold, carrying you another step closer to your goal of feeling better physically, mentally, emotionally, and spiritually. The changes will take some time, but believe in yourself even when you don't feel you can. *Your subconscious hears and believes everything you say, so feed it positive, constructive thoughts.*

Your Unique Purpose

Have you considered your life purpose? If it's just to "enjoy the ride," then it won't really matter much what you do with your life. You'll coast along, hoping things will somehow work out. If you think your reason for existence is to make the most money you can, you will climb the career ladder—even if that career does not represent your true calling.

But if you believe God created you for a specific and unique purpose, you will want to know how to live out that mission consistently and effectively. God's Word says that you do it by *renewing your mind* daily: "Do not conform to the pattern of this world, but be transformed by the renewing of your mind. Then you will be able to test and approve what God's will is—his good, pleasing and perfect will" (Romans 12:2). When seeking to align your thoughts with God's will, you'll begin to recognize his calling for your life and the way he equips you to fulfill it.

When you live with purpose and conviction, you will not be easily upended when temptation comes your way. And you will be strengthened to achieve health and healing, drawing courage and perseverance from the fact that you are pursuing a high calling. Instead of getting off track, you will reaffirm the direction and intention of your life.

YOUR SUBCONSCIOUS HEARS AND BELIEVES EVERYTHING YOU SAY, SO FEED IT POSITIVE, CONSTRUCTIVE THOUGHTS.

The Old Testament prophet Jeremiah includes these words in his book: "'For I know the plans I have for you,' declares the LORD, 'plans to prosper you and not to harm you, plans to give you hope and a future'" (29:11).

Those are words given to you and to me. God does indeed have plans for us—and hope and a future. That's fabulous news, and I want you to believe it with every fiber of your being. When we believe in our exciting, positive future, we have a reason to renew our thoughts according to God's will for our lives.

Purpose Is Essential to Health and Healing

Many people hear the word *purpose* and think it applies only to grand, world-changing work. Not necessarily. Purpose is the *unique thing* we each have to offer the world, no matter how big or small. It is a matter of investing your gifts and talents to benefit a nation or a neighborhood, a community or a classroom, a whole company or a single child. Your personal purpose may be to raise healthy children or invest in the lives of your grandchildren. It may be to help homeless people get off the streets and back on their feet. It might be to create art that inspires others. The possibilities are endless, and only you can know which best fits you.

> **FINDING AND FOLLOWING YOUR PURPOSE IS ESSENTIAL TO HEALTH AND HEALING.**

Look back on your life and identify situations that brought you the most joy, fulfillment, and gratification. Review your experiences and listen when you hear yourself say, *I absolutely loved doing that!* Think deeply as you ponder these statements:

■ What brings me to life more than anything is

_____.

■ I never feel more energized than when I

_____.

■ The best gift I can give to the world is

_____.

■ The need that stirs my soul more than any other is

_____.

Finding and following your purpose is essential to health and healing. Why? Because it's what keeps you going when you want to give up. It's what renews your energy after an exhausting week. It's what brings joy to your hurting heart.

Cultivate Gratitude

Gratitude is the antidote for toxic things that come into our lives. Simply put, gratitude fosters optimism, which strengthens hope. That's why it's hard to imagine more effective soul medicine than gratitude. The list of things we can and should be thankful for—even in our darkest moments—is practically inexhaustible.

Granted, sometimes troubles make it hard to muster gratitude for things like being alive or the loved ones in your life. So begin with small ones. Try saying thanks for crisp leaves on a fall day, the taste of your favorite tea, the phone call from your best friend, or the chance to sleep in on a Saturday morning.

Gratitude has a way of spreading exponentially. The more you choose to be grateful, the more you will find to appreciate. You will notice the beauty all around you in the world, and you will develop an acute awareness of the loving God responsible for it all. When dark thoughts threaten to push everything else aside, purposeful gratitude is a powerful way to push back.

Gratitude can be a sign of spiritual maturity. People who recognize their blessings and give thanks for them are living the essence of happiness, health, and healing.

Let me tell you a tale of two men. Ben and Howard were both elderly when I met them. They had known each other since birth, grew up in the same town, and attended the same college. Ben came from a wealthy family, so tuition for his education was paid by his parents. Howard worked his way through school as a carpenter.

After graduation, Ben attended law school and became a successful attorney. He was active in politics and served two terms in the state legislature. When he retired, Ben was a wealthy and powerful man. For him, the American dream lived up to its material promise.

PEOPLE WHO RECOGNIZE THEIR BLESSINGS AND GIVE THANKS FOR THEM ARE LIVING THE ESSENCE OF HAPPINESS, HEALTH, AND HEALING.

Howard dreamed of starting his own business after college. But when his father died suddenly, Howard left school to support his mother and younger siblings. Before he knew it, he had a mortgage and a family of his own. He worked hard but always struggled financially. His first house was destroyed by a fire. His daughter died of leukemia at age sixteen. By any measurement, Howard's life had been a series of tragedies and shattered dreams.

When I met them, one of these men was contented and happy. He had a smile and a kind word for everyone he met. Most days, his house was filled with the sounds of laughing grandchildren.

The other man was cynical and resentful. He hadn't spoken with his only son in years. He spent a lot of time alone because few people wanted to hear about his disappointments—again. He surrounded himself in an uninviting atmosphere of regret, anger, and sorrow.

You've probably guessed by now that Howard, who had many reasons to complain, was joyful and at peace. Ben was bitter, despite his advantages.

ACCEPTANCE AND GRATITUDE OPEN THE DOORS FOR YOU TO EXPERIENCE THE FULLNESS OF LIFE.

I once asked Ben how he felt about his life. No matter how successful he was in court, he couldn't rest until he'd won the next big case. As a state representative, he had kept an eye on a congressional seat or the governor's mansion. What he had was never enough.

This is how Howard answered the same question: "I tried to live by what my grandmother taught me when I was a young boy. She said the key to happiness was not to get what you want, but to want what you get. She had a hard life, but when she gave thanks for what she had, you knew she meant it."

Acceptance and gratitude open the doors for you to experience the fullness of life and a heart of peace. Closely observe the countless good things you enjoy but may tend to overlook. Spend time intentionally cultivating gratitude and watch how it improves everything about your life.

Finding God-given blessings in every situation and each day is one of the indispensable keys to bouncing back, being resilient, and achieving optimal health. On the other hand, when a spirit of ingratitude takes root in our hearts—no matter the reason—it can be difficult to recognize and hard to release.

INCREASE YOUR TQ

We need to learn that a high TQ (thankfulness quotient) is going to make us happier, help us enjoy life more, and foster healing in every way. I believe a high intelligence quotient (IQ) gives people advantages in life, and I know that a high emotional intelligence (EQ) enables people to excel personally and professionally. But I've become convinced that a high TQ will add to the quality of our lives like nothing else.

If you have been wounded, it may seem wise to venture out cautiously and carefully. Pessimism *appears* to be the protective armor you need to engage in a hostile world. But though self-defense seems like a logical approach to the wounded person, pessimism leads to death—the death of optimism. A pessimistic attitude may fend off disappointment and potential pain, but it also impedes enthusiasm, joyfulness, genuine laughter, and trust in others.

Say No to Negativity

Thankfully, we all have access to hope and can choose hopefulness as our prevailing approach to life. This is the mental and emotional framework that supports happiness—even when the winds of negativity buffet it.

The source of hope is a gracious and loving God who is in this world.

But how do you make optimism the foundation of your life? How does happiness become the norm rather than the exception? The change from pessimism to optimism takes effort and practice. Your optimistic muscles have atrophied, while your pessimistic muscles are as pumped up as a bodybuilder's.

THE SOURCE OF HOPE IS A GRACIOUS AND LOVING GOD WHO IS IN THIS WORLD.

Begin with small steps. For every pessimistic thought, worry, or fear that comes to mind, intentionally stop and search for a positive, optimistic response. Deliberately replace discouraging thoughts with encouraging ones.

It is possible to learn to live above your circumstances. Do you know someone whose attitude is amazing, even though they've gone through terrible things in life? Do you know someone whose well-being seems to be impervious to the ups and downs of daily life? These optimists have one thing in common: They make the daily *choice* to look for the good in life, even amid difficult circumstances.

If you do have a friend like this, be assured that that person is not in denial. Just the opposite is true. In order to shake off the chains of negativity, we must begin with the truth. When we acknowledge and then accept our circumstances, we begin to allow God into the process.

The negative voices in your head will not go away overnight. Invite God to help you renew your mind, focus on the positive things in your life, and tune out the negative thoughts you *can* control.

We can only live above our circumstances when we surrender control into the hands of a loving God who will lift us up and carry us forward.

HEALTHY THOUGHTS, HELPFUL CHOICES

How tall will a tree grow? I'm sure you agree that it will grow as tall as it's been designed by God to grow. Trees don't think in terms of limits. They just keep growing and growing because it's what they do naturally.

Apply this same process to every aspect of your life. Don't think *limits*—think *growth*. Think of the exciting possibilities that are ahead for you.

You have hundreds of choices each day—what time to get up in the morning, what internet sites to check, what food to eat, what to-do items to complete. How will you let your healthy thoughts lead to helpful choices today? Reaching out to someone new? Calling someone you haven't spoken to for many years? Asking someone for their forgiveness?

The possibilities are endless, so pick some things to pursue with all the enthusiasm your heart can muster. Tree growth isn't limited—and neither are your healthy thoughts.

Heal *Your* Emotions

I'm sure you've heard the phrase that someone was "so angry they couldn't see straight." I thought it was a colorful cliché—just another way of saying someone was really upset—until the first time it happened to me.

I don't remember now why I was so angry. But I distinctly remember the surprise I felt when fury temporarily distorted my vision.

I'm sure you know what it feels like to be flooded with strong and overwhelming emotions. Perhaps you've experienced this level of anger. Or grief. Or anxiety.

Sometimes the emotions that haunt us don't come in a flood, but in a never-ending slow drip we can't escape. Something in our past caused us to feel hurt, vulnerable, bitter, or ashamed . . . and now we live regularly with that emotion.

Emotions are a part of life—and a healthy life, at that. But a painful emotion can develop a life of its own by becoming a permanent resident in our emotional landscape. A painful emotion can impair our ability to function, making us feel trapped and without hope—and it's a sign that something needs to be healed.

Deal *with* Toxic Emotions

When I was growing up, my friends and I played outside for hours. I can remember summer days that seemed to last forever. Running around our neighborhood barefoot, living in the moment, our only concern was when we might hear our mothers calling us home for dinner as darkness fell. Those days seemed utterly carefree. Many of us look back wistfully on the unhurried days of childhood and wonder how our lives have become so complicated, burdensome, and stressful.

If you are feeling stressed to the point of burnout or on the threshold of emotional exhaustion, the main culprits contributing to your troubles are likely anger, fear, and guilt. These emotions are inescapable—we all experience them. Our challenge is to not let these normal emotions spin out of control and become toxic.

IT'S IMPORTANT TO KNOW THE DIFFERENCE BETWEEN HEALTHY AND UNHEALTHY EXPRESSIONS OF ANGER, FEAR, AND GUILT.

Life is filled with difficult people and challenging circumstances, some of which can cripple us emotionally. Those things can cause us to get angry—a natural response to hurt and intimidation. Then we become fearful, wondering if we've done the right thing by expressing our red-hot feelings. So we back off

and deny our anger, become a captive to our fears, and begin to live with guilt for having taken a stand in the first place.

It seems that we're always living with this emotionally toxic trinity: *anger, fear,* and *guilt.* They become particularly troublesome when we hang on to these emotions long after they should have done their useful work. It's important to know the difference between *healthy* and *unhealthy* expressions of anger, fear, and guilt. How you handle these often-poisonous emotions will be a major key to your regaining control and emotional balance.

Unproductive Anger

Have you ever seen those celebrations where people shoot weapons straight into the air? I often wonder where the bullets land! Anger can be like that. We feel justified, so we lose our cool, shoot off our mouth (which can be as damaging as a misused firearm), and immediately feel better. But the "bullets" of anger and hate that we launch will return to hurt us every time.

Sometimes our anger is uncalled for, inappropriate, and a hazard to our physical and emotional health. How do we avoid those misfires? A good strategy is to recognize wrong beliefs you may have about someone's words or actions and how they affect you. By trying to look beneath the surface of the situation, understanding the other person's motivation and your reactions, you may be able to stand down before you fire off a round of self-destructive anger.

Avoiding Damage

Long-held anger and resentment are not only crippling for us emotionally, they may also be harmful to our physical health. Here are four ways to avoid the self-inflicted wounds of anger before they do damage:

1. **Be your own person.** Don't let the actions of anger enslave you and dictate how you feel. Pause and let your anger subside until you have a clear enough head to evaluate the situation mindfully.

2. **Don't intimidate, and don't be intimidated.** Be assertive by asking the person to be reasonable in your debate, even as you promise to return the favor.

3. **If the shoe fits, wear it.** Before you raise your defenses, ask God to give you the courage to accept the truth and confess your fault, if necessary.

4. **Practice intentional kindness.** God's Word says that a kind word turns away anger (Proverbs 15:1). Your tone—in voice and body posture—can help diffuse an otherwise volatile situation.

Banish Fear of Failure

A distracted driver forces you off the road, and you react to avert disaster. In that case, fear is a good thing. Or consider guilt: If we have done hurtful things in our lives, that realization may drive us toward God and to a place of accepting his forgiveness. In this case, the guilt for legitimately bad things in our pasts spurred us toward redemption.

FAILURES ARE EVENTS, NOT PEOPLE.

However, a great majority of the time, fear and guilt fester deep inside our minds and emotions like an infection.

The truth is, we all make mistakes. Sometimes we fail miserably. We don't keep our promises. We see our lives as land mines of disaster. All this makes us angry, fearful, and ravaged with guilt.

So when you make a mistake, *feel* the anger, fear, or guilt. Then admit it, confess it, make amends, and move on. Evaluate your choices, knowing you are forgiven, healed, and whole in God's eyes. Recognize that today is a new day.

Failures are events, not people. Be kinder to yourself. Enter the freshness of God's love; open your heart to his unshakable goodness, his forgiveness of your sins, and his redeeming love.

Over time, you will say goodbye to the poisons of anger, fear, and guilt, because you will learn to use them properly. And what better time to start doing this than today!

Accentuate Acceptance

Knowledge is usually gained as insight. The lightbulb comes on, a puzzle piece falls into place, two halves come together to make a whole. In that moment, you recognize the truth, and it becomes a part of you.

Accepting the truth, however, isn't always easy. Oh, you may hear the truth, but it doesn't seem to "fit well." It just feels wrong, even though you know it is right. Here are some examples:

- It can be hard to accept that those who should have loved you, in fact, didn't.

- It's challenging to accept that the way you've always viewed yourself isn't accurate.

- It's difficult to accept that your life was changed in significant ways by wrong things in your life—some things done by you and some done by others.

On the path to healing, *acceptance* allows you to move beyond the blockades of bitterness and blaming others. These roadblocks leave you stranded. And no matter how hard you push against them, they don't move. Because of the effort you're expending, it seems as if you're accomplishing something, but you're stuck—you're not moving forward to healing.

Don't Miss God's Grace

Most of the pain in our lives comes from the actions of others wounding us, and our own wrong choices compound the pain. To heal, we must learn the difference between the two.

But it's not enough to stop there. We must take the next step and accept what these wrong actions have done to our lives. And I believe the only way to accept this difficult truth is by applying grace. We must accept God's grace in our own lives and extend that grace to others.

If we were perfect people with perfect relationships, we wouldn't need grace. Truth wouldn't be difficult to accept, for it wouldn't contain the wreckage of troubled lives. In a flawed world, however, to accept ourselves and others, grace is imperative.

I've heard grace defined as "unmerited favor." If you don't have to do anything to earn it, then you can receive it without paying for it. You receive something you did not earn or deserve. Often, we think something free doesn't have much value. But in this case, the gift of grace extended to us from God is extremely valuable. The apostle Paul said, "For you know the generous act of our Lord Jesus Christ, that though he was rich, yet for your sakes he became poor, so that by his poverty you might become rich" (2 Corinthians 8:9 NRSV).

Like love and forgiveness, the concept of grace goes against our very nature. Grace is freely given, it cannot be earned, and it is extended to those who don't deserve it. Although grace is hard to understand, God means for us to have it and experience it.

The Power of Acceptance

When we are staring at a huge problem or trauma blocking our path, God's grace is the powerful force that pushes the obstacle out of the way. We aren't powerful enough to do it, but God is. An acceptance of God's grace allows us to put the past behind us.

But grace is much more than just erasing the past; it is about writing the future.

That's because when we are freed from the thicket of regret, blame, and shame, we can show grace to others in every situation. It's the ultimate form of "paying it forward." Only Jesus has already paid our tab.

Is God asking us to "act" perfect, as if our wounds never happened? Certainly not. It's about inviting him *into* the wound. As the Great Physician, he wants to apply his healing to your heart and mind. It is a process; sometimes it is instantaneous, and other times the healing takes much longer.

Spiritual acceptance is a trust process. When you do surrender your past, and give God your wounds, he will be faithful to join you in the journey of restoration. Along the way, his love will begin to replace the pain in your heart. So much so that you will have an excess, and that extra love will spill out of your life and into the lives of others.

Find Freedom in Forgiveness

As you've read the previous pages, you've probably detected a pattern—a roadmap—for your healing journey. You start with truth and continue to acceptance of grace. It is important to keep going, because one of your most important destinations is just ahead: forgiveness.

Why is forgiveness a desirable destination? It is the place where you experience freedom from the burden of your own wrongdoing and from bondage to the wrongdoing of others. Without that freedom, you will continue to carry anger, guilt, fear, and shame. These unwelcome companions will weigh you down, wear you out, and weaken your resolve to keep moving forward to healing.

Choose Acceptance and Trust God

Forgiveness comes down to an issue of acceptance and trust. Acceptance of the fact that God will forgive our mistakes, and trust that there is freedom in extending forgiveness to those who have wronged us. Often, we have the hardest time releasing ourselves from the regret of our past decisions and wrong life choices. Are you willing to accept and trust in God's forgiveness? If you trust him, then those sins you want to hold on to are already forgiven because of his love for you. Let them go!

WE CAN ONLY LIVE PEACEFULLY WHEN WE ACCEPT GOD'S FORGIVENESS OF OUR OWN MISTAKES.

We can only live peacefully when we accept God's forgiveness of our own mistakes. We are then called to extend our forgiveness to others.

God will give you the ability—in his power—to forgive others, even if they have grievously wronged you. He sees your pain, and by receiving his forgiveness (for yourself, and then by extending it to others), the miracle of grace becomes real for you.

For Maximum Health, Minimize Stress

Has modern technology and your ability to access infinite amounts of information and entertainment brought less stress or more stress into your life? Notice I did not say "more convenience" but "more stress."

Sure, we can buy everything we want online—clothes, computers, and cars—and yes, it's convenient. But has it made our lives more peaceful?

Most of us would agree that emotional energy has become a precious commodity in our lives. When we feel emotionally depleted, then anxiety and stress are the natural by-products. Left unchecked, stress can lead to feelings of being out of control.

As a result, stress can prompt us to seek temporary relief in unhealthy habits that create *more* stress in the long

run. Turning to alcohol, comfort food, or overspending might provide temporary relief and distraction, but these things greatly complicate our lives.

Not everything that causes us stress can be eliminated—nor should it. Low-level stress stimulates the brain to boost productivity and concentration. It can also be a big motivator to make changes, solve problems, or accomplish goals.

In addition, many sources of stress are simply beyond our control. That said, there are plenty of stressors we *can* control. Here are seven good strategies for you to begin practicing immediately:

1. IDENTIFY YOUR STRESSORS.

Make a list of the factors in your life that contribute to your stress, which might include:

- Relationship tension and troubles

- Overcommitment issues

- Unhealthy habits you use to escape or avoid dealing with issues

- Past regrets that affect the present

- Unhelpful ways of thinking and processing

- Lack of forgiveness for others or yourself

By understanding what creates stress in your life, you can begin to address those things and move toward healing.

2. STOP PROCRASTINATING.

This is a simple—though not easy—way to relieve pressure. Whether you are an occasional procrastinator or a serial procrastinator, your delays and avoidance amp up your stress levels.

3. KEEP YOUR BALANCE.

Protecting your time from overcommitments that are within your control isn't easy, but it's one of the most effective things you can do to reduce stress.

4. AVOID NEGATIVE ESCAPES.

When we are stressed, it's tempting to turn to excessive eating, spending, or substance abuse. That's because we want to do something to change our mood! Of course, the list of unhelpful and unhealthy escapes could go on and on. Negative escapes only spread the negativity throughout your entire life.

5. ESCAPE IN A HEALTHY WAY.

Thankfully, not all escapes are negative or destructive. In fact, taking a mental and emotional break from the source of stress is a powerful way to improve how you cope, transform your perspective, and help you identify long-term solutions. An escape could be as simple as spending an hour with an enjoyable book in a backyard hammock, or as elaborate as planning a trip to another state.

6. BREAK OUT OF ISOLATION.

Study after study show that supportive relationships are essential to improving how we experience and process stress. In fact, loneliness is linked not only to depression, but also health problems including high blood pressure, cardiovascular disease, cancer, and cognitive decline. Other studies show that people who are involved in faith communities tend to have lower levels of anxiety and stress.

7. TAKE GOOD CARE OF YOUR BODY.

One of the best things you can do to handle the stresses of life is to fortify your health and body. Eating right, getting enough sleep, and exercising regularly relieve feelings of stress and anxiety, improve your mood, and energize your body, brain, and emotions.

It's impossible to eliminate all stress from your life. Managing stress is another matter entirely. How much stress you experience—and how you respond when you experience it—are things you have more control over than you may realize.

The Ultimate Cure for Anxiety

"DO NOT BE ANXIOUS ABOUT ANYTHING, BUT IN EVERY SITUATION, BY PRAYER AND PETITION, WITH THANKSGIVING, PRESENT YOUR REQUESTS TO GOD. AND THE PEACE OF GOD, WHICH TRANSCENDS ALL UNDERSTANDING, WILL GUARD YOUR HEARTS AND YOUR MINDS IN CHRIST JESUS."
(PHILIPPIANS 4:6-7)

SEVEN WAYS TO EXPERIENCE INNER PEACE

It's become so commonplace for people to feel stressed and overloaded that we tend to forget there is an alternative way to live. It's time to slow down and consider ways to bring more peace to your heart and soul. Start with these ideas:

1. Beware of peace pickpockets.

You encounter all kinds of people and situations that try to steal your serenity. Know what they are and take measures to fend them off.

2. Take a mental-health day, or morning, or moment.

Whatever time you can allow, give yourself the space to refresh your mind and spirit.

3. Rethink your "should do" and "ought to do" lists.

If the voice in your head is guilting you into doing things that don't bring you joy, regard these as prime candidates to delete.

4. Kick the approval habit.

It's natural to want to be liked by others—and it's healthy to accept that it's not going to happen all the time.

5. Be still.

If your pace is wearing you out, set aside a half-day or a full day to sit on the sofa to think, journal, read, and nap.

6. Let music move you.

Few things are as cathartic and cleansing as your best-loved music. Use your favorite tunes to calm you down, pump you up, or stir your emotions.

7. Give yourself a quality-of-life checkup.

It's wise to periodically assess whether you're satisfied with the quality of your life. If you don't feel fulfilled, ponder what changes are in order.

Nurture *Your* Relationships

"*Love* makes the world go 'round," or so say the lyrics to a song made popular by the Broadway musical *Carnival!*

But the songwriter wasn't the first to recognize the power of relationships in our lives. In 1624, John Donne, a Renaissance priest and poet, penned the words, "No man is an island, entire of itself."

And earlier still—about 1000 BC—King Solomon wrote, "Two are better than one, because they have a good return for their labor: If either of them falls down, one can help the other up. But pity anyone who falls and has no one to help them up." (Ecclesiastes 4:9–10). We are social creatures—designed that way by our Creator—and the health of our relationships impacts every facet of life.

Even science agrees. Dr. Matthew Lieberman is a professor and Social Cognitive Neuroscience Lab Director at UCLA, as well as the author of the book *Social*. According to Dr. Lieberman, studies show that we are "profoundly shaped by our social environment and that we suffer greatly when our social bonds are threatened or severed." He adds, "We may not like the fact that we are wired such that our well-being depends on our connections with others, but the facts are the facts."[1]

We can't escape the fact that we need relationships—and that if we are to experience healthy, happy lives, we want those relationships to be as positive and healthy as possible.

Create *and* Maintain Healthy Relationships

I began this book by asserting that your self-talk—all the messages flowing through your brain—is the most essential aspect of determining the quality of your life. Running a close second as the most important and influential part of your life are your relationships. The people in your life contribute significantly to your well-being (or lack thereof).

We constantly use relationships to determine our position in life. We observe the people around us and make decisions about who we are based on how we believe others perceive us. That's why it's important to do all we can to maintain our healthy relationships and improve our unhealthy ones. A healthy relationship requires that each person bring something unique and special to it. A healthy relationship happens when two people understand and appreciate each other. A healthy relationship exists when value is placed not only on who you are together, but also on who you are individually.

Healthy people are growing people, and people do not grow healthy in isolation. We need each other for so many reasons: for companionship, encouragement, support, feedback, and insight.

Ten Traits of a Healthy Relationship

Relationships can be complicated and complex. Sometimes we become so close to a situation—and so intertwined with a person—that it's difficult to gauge whether a relationship is healthy or unhealthy. Whether you want to evaluate a marriage, friendship, family relationship, or any other personal connection, look for the following ten qualities, which are sure signs of strength and security:

1. TRUST

Two people develop trust because each has proven to be trustworthy and reliable. When tempted to betray the relationship in some way, they have held fast to the needs and feelings of the other person instead.

2. AUTHENTICITY

This means being who you truly are, resisting the impulse to play games or put on a false persona to impress someone. Authentic people aren't so judgmental, uptight, and defensive that they bristle at differences. They value individuality and uniqueness. In short, authenticity means being real and genuine in any circumstance.

3. HONESTY

One of the hallmarks of healthy friendships is living within an atmosphere of truth-telling. Being honest, however, does not entail a harsh, brutal presentation of someone's flaws. Instead, the truth should be spoken in love, compassion, and tenderness. To a friend, the truth is not a weapon; it is a healing balm. There is safety in the honest words of a friend, even when those words hurt.

4. UNDERSTANDING

A healthy relationship involves two people who know the background and context of each other's lives. They know *the what* of things, but they also know *the why* of things.

5. ACCEPTANCE

Friends understand the precarious position they put themselves in by being a friend. Proximity sometimes results in pain where human beings are concerned. Healthy people acknowledge this pain as an acceptable consequence of the relationship.

6. MUTUAL BENEFIT

True friends add to each other's lives. Often the benefit isn't always equal, but it is mutual. True friends monitor the relationship to ensure there is both give and take, refusing to allow it to become chronically one-sided and draining.

7. RESPECT

Mutual respect is at the very core of enduring relationships. It confers dignity, honor, and high worth to the recipient. In contrast, lack of respect leads to all kinds of relational ills—put-downs, dishonesty, cheating—which are sure to sink a relationship eventually.

8. UNSELFISHNESS

This quality is central to any healthy, harmonious relationship. If the person you're with shows little regard for your wishes and opinions, consistently puts their desires before anyone else's, and seems thoughtless and uncaring about others, you're probably in the presence of someone more selfish than selfless, more bigheaded than bighearted.

9. AFFECTION

At the heart of all friendships should be genuine affection. Friends enjoy each other. They like to be together because of the way they feel about each other.

10. JOYFULNESS

Healthy relationships involve two people who regularly laugh together, find reasons to celebrate, and experience delight in unexpected moments. It sounds simple, but the relationships that flourish include individuals who truly enjoy being together.

If you have most—or all—of these qualities in your relationship, be assured that your relationship is headed in the right direction . . . toward a satisfying, successful future.

Surround Yourself with Life-Giving People

Have you ever felt that you were letting other people determine what kind of day you were going to have? If they were angry, you got angry. If they were happy, you jumped on the same happy wagon.

Psychologists call this phenomenon "emotional contagion" or "mood transference," which is described as having one person's emotions directly trigger similar emotions in other people. If brief encounters with others' emotions can influence us so strongly, just imagine the long-term effects of the people we spend time with on a regular basis. Each of those interactions accumulate over time to help shape us into who we are.

THE MOST FULFILLED RELATIONSHIPS INVOLVE PEOPLE WHO GENUINELY WANT EACH OTHER TO EXPERIENCE A LIFE OF HAPPINESS, MEANING, AND FULFILLMENT.

It matters tremendously who we allow into our lives! We can't always select the people who fill our lives, but in most instances, we *can* choose who to get close to and who to keep our distance from.

Think for a moment about the people whose company you value and cherish. Recall those who make a positive difference in your life. They are interested in you and invested in you. They share their lives with you and encourage you to do the same. They pick you up when you fall.

The most fulfilled marriage relationships, dating relationships, and friendships involve people who genuinely want each other to experience a life of happiness, meaning, and fulfillment. They offer continual encouragement and look for practical ways to help the other person excel. It is this collective strength that contributes to the greatness of a supportive, mutual relationship.

As we find friends who will challenge us to something better, support us in all our attempts, and cheer us in our achievements, we need to deepen those relationships. We all need people around us who will, without being judgmental, call us to a bigger, bolder life—who will help us move out of our comfort zones and take giant steps forward. We need people who will accept us for who we are and challenge us to pursue our goals with energy and determination.

Guard against Joy-Stealers

Just as we should be intentional about inviting supportive people into our lives, we need to be equally intentional about guarding against people who tear us down.

Healthy boundaries keep toxic people from undermining the passionate life you want to live. The less you allow an invasion of the joy-stealers, the less poison you will take into your own system.

I'd like you to put up a mental "boundary crossing" sign to help remind you where people may have overstepped their privileges in the past—and may even continue to do so in the present. It may be well-meaning but negative family influences. It may be some form of emotional or physical abuse that you've allowed to rule your life, making you feel inadequate and distracting you from reaching your potential. Summon the courage to hold firm boundaries with manipulative or mean-spirited people—because your health and healing are well worth it.

SIX WAYS TO STRENGTHEN YOUR RELATIONSHIPS

The best relationships continue to develop and grow when the two people involved refuse to settle for mediocrity or monotony. If you want your relationship with someone to go from good to great, employ these key practices:

1. Approach the person with an attitude of gratefulness.

If this person is a significant part of your life, let him or her know it. Express your appreciation freely and frequently.

2. Allow for differences.

People enjoy being able to express their unique thoughts, opinions, and feelings, knowing they will be received with an open mind and heart by the listener. Interacting in this way will give you the opportunity to truly understand the other person.

3. Be respectful of the boundaries he/she feels are necessary for the relationship.

If you want the other person to honor your boundaries, you must do the same.

4. Ask forgiveness when you make a mistake.

Don't try to hide your blunder. And don't try to magnify or minimize it—just be truthful and straightforward.

5. Exercise forgiveness yourself.

When the other person apologizes for a misdeed, extend grace and compassion.

6. Be quick to resolve conflicts.

Disagreements are inevitable in any relationship and shouldn't be avoided. Instead, in a spirit of unity, you and the other person should talk through the issue, explain your positions, and come to a resolution.

Find Accountability Partners *to* Propel *You* Forward

Each of us needs someone with whom we are fully accountable. This is a person who knows us, accepts us, loves us, and will be honest with us. How does this idea strike you?

In our individualistic, isolated society, many people like to "go it alone," with an attitude that says, "I don't need anyone poking around in my life. I'm doing just fine on my own."

WHEN WE ARE NOT ACCOUNTABLE FOR OUR OWN ACTIONS, WE MAKE CHOICES THAT HINDER OUR GROWTH.

But often these people are not really doing "just fine." When we are not accountable for our own actions, we make choices that hinder our growth and thwart our progress. One of your greatest fears may be of "being known" by

another person. Yet, without facing this fear, you may be missing out on some of God's greatest blessings in your life.

Many people resist the idea of being accountable because they misunderstand what that word means. Accountability is not about judgment, retribution, keeping score, or being controlled. Nor does it mean handing over to someone else more power or influence than they should have. In truth, accountability is . . .

- The willingness to invite someone—a trusted someone—to see into your life, even the places you would prefer to keep hidden.

- The practice of vulnerability and honesty, being willing to tell the truth, and being receptive to feedback—even when the truth may be uncomfortable.

- The determination to take specific healthy action, without excuse or regret.

- The purposeful decision to be your very best self, with the help of someone who will come alongside to share your journey.

When we feel we are damaging the quality of our lives with destructive habits or harmful choices, this is usually the first sign of a need to change and to begin taking responsibility for our lives. But we're usually not strong enough to do it alone. That's why we need nonjudgmental, supportive people who will ask us tough questions and support us through the agreed-upon actions.

Let's say your struggle is a bad temper that results in explosive outbursts, often at people you love. You yell at your children, berate your spouse, and lose your cool with friends. Of course, you know this is not respectful, healthy behavior, and you desperately want to change.

In confidence, you share your problem with your friends, and you ask them to be your supporters and partners as you determine to make serious changes in your actions and anger management. This may seem risky, even scary. But there can be neither growth nor meaningful change without some form of risk.

Here are some specifics of what makes a healthy, helpful accountability relationship:

1. You must trust your friends implicitly and choose to be accountable to them, which always means telling them the truth and allowing them to give you honest feedback.

2. Your partners are not to serve as "rescuers." You are not looking for people who will become codependent, taking responsibility for you and your conduct. *You* are responsible for you, and your partners are intended to be encouragers, guides, and truth-tellers.

3. The arrangement should not involve any "power dynamics." You and God are your sole authorities. Only as you become aware of the person God designed you to be will you be motivated and empowered to reach your potential.

4. Plan your accountability around *specific* issues and goals. These relationships should not try to tackle *anything and everything*, nor should they become unfocused and ambiguous. You and your accountability partner should know precisely why you have joined together in this effort. For example, you might want a partner to help you begin a daily exercise regimen over the next three months—and you can check in with the other person several times a week to report your progress.

We were never intended to be islands, alone amid a sea of confusion. That's why I encourage you to find those people who will help you grow by keeping you accountable.

Build Fulfilling Relationships *by* Being Fully Present

Woody Allen once quipped, "Eighty percent of success is showing up." Unfortunately, many people apply that line of reasoning to their relationships. They think that just "being there" is enough to ensure relational harmony.

I don't think so. Physical presence is a completely different matter than emotional, mental, and spiritual presence. Your body may be sitting right next to your partner, but your mind can be a thousand miles away.

ONE OF THE GREATEST GIFTS OF LOVE WE CAN GIVE ANOTHER PERSON IS TO BE FULLY PRESENT IN BODY, MIND, AND SPIRIT.

Connor and Erica came to me for marriage counseling. He was a successful businessman trying to keep up with endless details and demands. She was a neglected wife who wanted more from their relationship.

At one point, Connor said, "Look, I've cut way back on my work hours, and I'm home each night by six-thirty. We have dinner together almost every evening. What more do you want?"

"I appreciate all the changes you've made," Erica responded. "A lot of times, though, I feel like you're distracted. Even when you're 'with me,' you're not *with* me. We sit together at the dinner table, but there might as well be a continent separating us. Many times, you nod and say 'uh-huh,' but I know you're not listening."

Connor, though physically present, wasn't tuned in to his wife. His body was at home while his brain was at the office. Erica would enjoy her marriage much more—and so would Connor—if they could learn to be present together.

In his book *Catching the Rhythm of Love*, psychologist Neil Clark Warren says:

> The secret of cultivating love is maximizing the number of life experiences in which you and your partner are deeply captured by a momentary or lasting event. When I say, "deeply captured," I mean that the event exists right at the center of

your thoughts and feelings. If both of you are focused on one experience, and if your focus of consciousness includes both the event and your partner, the power of this moment to stimulate love between you will be maximal.[1]

There is something irresistible about being with someone who is fully and completely present—all attention and energy focused like a laser beam on *you*. Indeed, this is one of the greatest gifts of love we can give another person: to be *fully present* in body, mind, and spirit. This sends an overwhelmingly powerful message to the person you're with: "You are more important and more valuable to me than anything else in the world."

Next time you are with your spouse or dating partner or close friend, practice this approach. Intentionally be present with this person, concentrating as much as possible on their words, gestures, voice intonation, and body language. Give them your full attention. Activate all your senses and be *right there* with them. Then evaluate what kind of magic transpires.

RECRUIT A MENTOR/COACH

Someone once said that we may not have come over on the same ship, but we're all in the same boat. And another of our many common features is that we all have a need for a relationship with someone who has the wisdom and love to serve as our mentor, our coach.

Here's what mentors do:

- Model a healthy lifestyle

- Encourage our healthy self-esteem

- Give us honest feedback to help us monitor our progress

- Challenge us to live our purpose and follow our passion

- Practice and encourage healthy boundaries

- Believe in our positive future

- Help us by leading the way and "living out" what we are becoming, even though they are not perfect

I encourage you to find your own mentor, who can help you thrive in every way as you pursue happiness, health, and healing.

Nourish *Your* Body

How well you take care of your body impacts your energy level, your physical health, and your emotions. It affects your self-esteem, your confidence, and even how well you think and perform mentally.

The quality of your experience as a spouse, parent, friend, or employee is influenced by how well you take care of your body. If treating your body poorly leaves you fatigued, sick, insecure, or depressed, it impacts nearly every facet of your life.

Perhaps you know you should take better care of yourself, but you have so many other priorities that it doesn't happen. Or maybe you understand the importance of regular exercise, but you can never find the time. Or it could be that you understand the importance and have the time, but you're a procrastinator and you keep putting it off.

Whatever your reasons, it's time for a change. I want to equip you with the reasons for making that change, as well as simple steps you can take that will get you well on your way to greater health and healing.

Nurture Yourself *with* Nutritious Foods

The psalmist had a poetic description of the human body, saying we were "fearfully and wonderfully made" by our Creator (Psalm 139:14). God designed our bodies and the earth's rich food sources to work in harmony, bringing us maximum health and wellness.

Nutritious, fortifying foods not only support physical health but mental health as well. What you put in your mouth each day directly and dramatically affects your mood and mental health.

Some of the main culprits leading to nutritional imbalance and potential depression and anxiety include:

1. Processed foods

2. Junk foods

3. White flour

4. Fried foods

5. Refined sugar

When your energy levels are down from anxiety or depression, these "quick" foods can be highly tempting and temporarily satisfying. But eating them is not a good strategy for combatting depression. Good, nutritious foods and beverages will improve your mood and sense of well-being.

Foods That Help Relieve "the Blues"

Here are several helpful strategies—along with specific food recommendations—that will enrich your body and lift your mood:

▪ ANTIOXIDANTS

By eating foods rich in antioxidants, you can diminish the destructive effects of free radicals (unstable atoms that can damage cells, causing illness and premature aging). Start with these:

- Beta-Carotene: apricots, broccoli, cantaloupe

- Vitamin C: blueberries, broccoli, potatoes

- Vitamin E: nuts and seeds, vegetable oils

▪ "COMPLEX" CARBS

Researchers have linked carbohydrates to serotonin, the mood-boosting brain chemical. It's speculated that craving carbs may be related to low serotonin activity. Target "smart" or "complex" carbs (such as whole grains) rather than simple carbs (such as cakes and cookies). Fruits, vegetables, and legumes also have healthy carbs and fiber.

HEALTHY PROTEINS

It's helpful to eat protein-rich foods several times a day, especially when your energy level needs a lift. These include beans and peas, lean beef, low-fat cheese, fish, milk, poultry, and yogurt.

B VITAMINS

Studies show that low levels of vitamins B1 and B12, along with folate, can exacerbate depression. You can get both B vitamins and folate from foods such as legumes, nuts, many fruits, and dark green vegetables. Vitamin B12 can be found in all lean and low-fat animal products, such as fish and low-fat dairy products.

■ VITAMIN D

Research has demonstrated a link between vitamin D deficiency and depression. Consume plenty of salmon, egg yolks, yogurt, whole milk, almond milk, orange juice, oatmeal, cheese, shiitake mushrooms, and fortified tofu.

■ SELENIUM

Studies have found a connection between low selenium and depression. Try to incorporate some of these foods into your diet: beans and legumes, lean meat (lean pork and beef, skinless chicken and turkey), low-fat dairy products, nuts and seeds, seafood (oysters, clams, sardines, crab, salt-water fish, and freshwater fish), and whole grains.

■ OMEGA-3 FATTY ACIDS

Researchers have discovered that societies not consuming enough omega-3s may have higher rates of major depressive disorder. Good sources of omega-3s include fatty fish (anchovy, mackerel, salmon, sardines, shad, and tuna; flaxseed; canola and soybean oils; nuts (especially walnuts); and dark green, leafy vegetables.

■ FIBER

Aim to replace high-sugar and high-fat foods with those high in fiber. This includes vegetables (particularly asparagus and Jerusalem artichokes), bananas, oatmeal, legumes and nuts, and grains such as barley, whole wheat, and oats.

■ CHOCOLATE

Studies have shown that dark chocolate increases the growth of two helpful bacteria strains in the body. Dark chocolate with 75 percent cacao or more may naturally lead you toward low-sugar treats.

Health and Hydration

Scientists have identified a strong connection between dehydration and depression, noting that even mild dehydration will affect your moods.

Drinking the right amount of water (not just liquids, but *water*) will help:

- Maintain proper balance of body fluids
- Aid in weight loss
- Energize muscles
- Support kidney function
- Assist with digestion
- Keep skin looking good

Drink the equivalent of half your body weight in ounces of water each day.

Steps toward a Better Mood

Let's look at some concrete steps you can take to improve your diet and help you overcome anxiety, depression, and other mood destabilizers.

1. Take the two-week food log challenge. Carefully track what you've been eating so you can spot areas for improvement and create better habits as you adjust your diet.

2. Conduct an inventory of your refrigerator and pantry to see how many foods you own that have sugars or sweeteners added.

3. Be extra vigilant on your upcoming shopping trips.

4. Lean on a support system. Getting healthy takes help—reach out to a friend or relative who can serve as an accountability partner.

5. Stop and intentionally evaluate how different you feel after four weeks on your new nutritional regimen.

Sleep Well

Remember when you were a kid, and after a big day at the amusement park you would fall asleep on the ride home? I can still remember that feeling of being half-awake as my dad carried me inside to my bed. It seems like kids can fall asleep anytime, anywhere.

As we get older, sleep can become a little trickier. In fact, studies show that more than a third of American adults—and more than two-thirds of teenagers—don't get enough sleep on a regular basis.

What may come as a surprise isn't just the pervasiveness of the problem, but one of the driving forces behind it: our ever-growing obsession with technology. According to a National Sleep Foundation poll, people who text in the hour before trying to fall asleep even a few nights a week are less likely to report getting a good night's sleep.[1]

A GOOD NIGHT'S SLEEP IS DETERMINED BY MANY CHOICES, HABITS, AND BEHAVIORS THROUGHOUT THE DAY.

There are several contributing factors to this problem. The phone itself wakes us up (texts, notifications, alerts, and so on); the shortwaves emitted by the light on our phones interferes with the body's natural production of melatonin; and technology right before sleep is both physiologically and psychologically stimulating.

Another influence on sleep problems is the rise in prescription drug use. Offending drugs can include medications related to past illnesses as well as concurrent illnesses. Antidepressants and anti-anxiety medications often have unwanted side effects.

Over-the-counter pain medications and decongestants have also been linked with insomnia.

When we don't get enough sleep, our bodies, brains, and emotions are impacted, and we can experience:

- Decreased overall activity in the brain

- Impaired driving performance

- Interference with healthy heart function

- Compromises in how our bodies repair joint and muscle injuries

- Reduced production of the hormones our bodies produce to control appetite, leading to increased obesity

- Greater cognitive and behavior issues experienced by people with dementia

A good night's sleep doesn't begin an hour or two before bed, but is determined by many choices, habits, and behaviors throughout the day. There are many things you can do during your waking hours that will greatly improve the quality of your sleep.

■ GET EXPOSURE TO NATURAL LIGHT.

Exposure to sunlight helps maintain a healthy sleep cycle. In fact, our bodies use intervals of light and darkness to determine our circadian rhythm, or internal clock.

■ EXERCISE.

As little as ten minutes of aerobic exercise during the day can dramatically improve nighttime sleep. Because rigorous exercise circulates endorphins throughout the body, which can make it harder to fall asleep, try getting your exercise in before midafternoon every day.

■ TAKE SHORT NAPS.

While napping doesn't make up for missed nightly sleep, a short nap of twenty to thirty minutes can improve mood, alertness, and performance. Try limiting daytime naps to a half hour so sleeping at night is not compromised.

■ REVIEW THE MEDICATIONS YOU ARE TAKING.

If you suspect that your sleep issues are related to a

certain medication you use, talk to your physician or pharmacist.

As Evening Approaches

▪ WATCH WHAT YOU EAT CLOSE TO BEDTIME.

It's no secret that heavy, rich, or spicy foods can keep you awake at night. When it comes to eating and drinking before bed, go easy on anything you consume.

▪ AVOID STIMULANTS CLOSE TO BEDTIME.

Coffee is an obvious stimulant, but many people forget that soda and tea can contain caffeine as well. Nicotine and exercise are other stimulants that can keep us from falling quickly into sleep. Emotionally upsetting conversations and activities also fall into this category. As discussed earlier, even something as innocuous as texting right before bed provides light and stimulation that can undermine the quality of your sleep.

▪ FOLLOW A REGULAR, RELAXING BEDTIME ROUTINE.

Your process might include taking a warm shower or bath, reading a book, or listening to soothing music. Your routine should also include going to bed and waking up around the same time each day.

■ CREATE A COMFORTABLE ENVIRONMENT.

As evening approaches, make sure you have arranged a peaceful, calming environment for sleeping. Things that may help create this environment could include a comfortable mattress, a cool bedroom, earplugs, white noise machines, humidifiers, and fans.

■ DON'T WATCH TV, STUDY, OR READ IN BED.

Just as regular, relaxing bedtime routines can help your brain and body know when it's time for sleep, your bed itself is another important trigger. By helping your brain associate your bed with sleep, the transition into slumber will be much smoother.

At Night

■ KEEP YOUR ROOM AS DARK AS POSSIBLE.

Remember, our bodies use exposure to light and dark to "set" our internal clocks. Even small amounts of light from lamps, cell phones, TV screens, and digital clocks can interfere.

▪ DON'T STAY IN BED AWAKE FOR MORE THAN FIVE TO TEN MINUTES.

Given the need to train our brains to associate our beds with sleeping, lying awake in bed for hours is rarely a good idea. Instead, if you can't fall back asleep within about ten minutes, get out of bed and sit in a chair in the dark until you feel sleepy. And whatever you do, don't pick up your phone to check Facebook or turn on the television. The light will confuse your internal clock and stimulate your brain.

As you seek to improve the quality of your sleep, you may find it helpful to photocopy or print the recommendations above and read them regularly. If you accidentally omit some of these recommendations, or have a bad night, don't be discouraged—just get back on track the next day. By continuing to follow these recommendations, you'll be establishing habits that will promote great sleep opportunities and emotional wellness.

Get Moving

Perhaps you've heard the phrase, "A rose by any other name would smell as sweet." As William Shakespeare intended in *Romeo and Juliet*, calling something by a different name doesn't change its essence.

That's the basic approach I take when I talk with those who are struggling and feel overwhelmed by the word *exercise*. Instead, I use the phrase "physical movement." Many depressed individuals have such low energy and low motivation that exercise is the last thing they want to do.

By starting slow, even just ten minutes a day, we give our bodies, routines, and self-discipline time to catch up to what our brains know we need to do. The important thing is to begin doing *something*, no matter how small or simple.

The idea that exercise can alleviate depression, stress, and anxiety is not a new one. Neither is the idea that, in some cases, exercise can be as effective as prescription medications in stabilizing or improving moods.

The Magic Hour

A study published in the *American Journal of Psychiatry* followed 33,908 healthy adults for eleven years and tracked data related to exercise, depression, and anxiety.[2] The researchers concluded that sedentary participants were 44 percent more likely to develop depression than participants who exercised just one to two hours a week. In fact, that "one-hour mark" was particularly significant. Here are some of the conclusions of the study:

■ When it came to protecting people from depression, most of the benefits were realized with an hour of low-level exercise per week.

■ Low-intensity exercises were just as beneficial as high-intensity exercises. Relatively modest increases in the overall amount of time spent exercising per week may be able to prevent a substantial number of new cases of depression. The benefits of even moderate physical activity are widespread and substantial. According to Dr. Alpa Patel, strategic director of the American Cancer Society's Cancer Prevention Study-3, "When you go from doing no activity to any amount, you see a marked decline in the risk of premature death from any cause." I am struck by that amazing sequence of words: *any amount . . . marked decline in . . . premature death from any cause.*

Of course, there are additional benefits from consistent workouts of higher intensity. According to the Physical Activity Guidelines for Americans, your weekly activity goal should include two and a half hours of moderate-intensity aerobic activity (such as brisk walking) and two days of muscle-strengthening activities that work all major muscle groups (legs, hips, back, abs, chest, shoulders, and arms).[3] Meeting these guidelines can literally save your life, creating dramatic improvements related to diabetes, heart health, bone and muscle strength, and more.[4]

How Physical Movement Helps Mental Health

Here are five critical chemicals and hormones that have a major impact on brain health and mood. They are all positively impacted through exercise:

1. NOREPINEPHRINE

Both a hormone and brain chemical, norepinephrine makes you more alert, while improving focus, memory, and concentration.

2. DOPAMINE

This is a neurotransmitter linked to pleasure and motivation. It also helps you plan, concentrate, and experience feelings of joy and accomplishment when you reach your goals.

3. SEROTONIN

This brain chemical is a natural mood stabilizer that significantly impacts your emotions, but it also helps regulate appetite, sleep, memory, sexual desire, and social behavior.

4. BRAIN-DERIVED NEUROTROPHIC FACTOR (BDNF)

This chemical promotes the growth of new connections between brain cells, making it extremely crucial to overall brain health. Exercise can triple the production of BDNF in your brain.

5. ENDORPHINS

These neurochemicals minimize discomfort and stress. They are, in fact, your brain's natural pain-killers, and they're linked to feelings of euphoria and general well-being.

Physical movement also helps to . . .

▪ STRENGTHEN BONES

Weight-bearing exercises strengthen bones by causing new bone tissue to grow. These include walking, jogging, climbing stairs, dancing, and even jumping. Non-weight-bearing exercises include swimming and bicycling.

▪ BUILD MUSCLES

Muscle-building exercises are increasingly im-portant as we age, as the human body begins losing muscle mass from about the age of thirty.

▪ PROVIDE A BETTER NIGHT'S SLEEP

According to one study, people with chronic insomnia who engaged in medium-intensity aerobic exercise (such as walking) fell asleep quicker and slept longer.

LOWER BLOOD SUGAR

Exercise lowers blood sugar by increasing insulin sensitivity. This helps your muscle cells use available insulin to take up glucose during and after your workout.

BOOST YOUR CREATIVITY

> God Cares about Your Whole Person
>
> "MAY GOD HIMSELF, THE GOD OF PEACE, SANCTIFY YOU THROUGH AND THROUGH. MAY YOUR WHOLE SPIRIT, SOUL AND BODY BE KEPT BLAMELESS AT THE COMING OF OUR LORD JESUS CHRIST." (1 THESSALONIANS 5:23)

Research conducted at Stanford University showed that something as simple as casual walking improves creativity by boosting convergent thinking (solving a problem), as well as divergent thinking (coming up with original ideas).[5]

HELP YOU COPE

Physical movement is not only a coping strategy that provides stress relief in the moment, but it also offers innumerable lasting benefits for a healthy brain and body.

■ ALTER YOUR ATTITUDE

Physical movement can be a game changer when it comes to your overall disposition and mindset.

■ SUPPORT CARDIOVASCULAR HEALTH

Four of the best exercises for a healthy heart are brisk walking, running, swimming, and bicycling.

Exercise is such a powerful resource because its impact is so comprehensive. The power of movement can become a catalyst for transformation in many areas of your life.

Six Steps toward a Better Lifestyle

Here are six ways to reap the long-term benefits of a more active life:

1. MAKE MOVEMENT FUN

Many people resist exercise because it sounds like drudgery—pounding the pavement with a beet-red face and sweat pouring down. That's why it's important to find something you enjoy doing, so you'll look forward to moving every day.

2. KEEP A JOURNAL

As you develop an exercise regimen, write about

any improvements you feel in your body, attitude, or emotions.

3. BE CONSISTENT

Especially as you get started, remember that consistency is more important than intensity.

4. BAN "ALL OR NOTHING" THOUGHTS

Consistency and commitment are indeed essential for an effective activity regimen—but don't be hard on yourself if you slack off a bit.

5. ENLIST THE HELP OF FITNESS APPS

Downloading a fitness app on your phone or purchasing an activity tracker isn't necessary but can be motivating for some people.

6. CREATE A FAVORITE WORKOUT PLAYLIST

Music and movement are a powerful combination.

Deepen *Your* Spirit

Just as we were created to take control of our thoughts, have a healthy range of emotions, be social beings, and fuel our bodies well, we were also created with a soul that needs care and attention in order to thrive.

The idea of deepening your spiritual life may sound nebulous, but it's not. There are specific things you can do that will help you strengthen areas in your spiritual life. This will prove to be an invaluable resource as you seek to experience greater health, happiness, and healing.

Seek Spiritual Intimacy

In a world of unsteady relationships, God's steadfast love keeps us on firm emotional and spiritual ground.

In a world of good-byes, God's presence can be a continual reminder of his love and care for us.

One thing I love about God is how he accepts and shapes us even when our relationships with others are broken. God doesn't deny the voids that are created when death, separation, and loss occur. Rather, he acknowledges the reality of our new shape and works within us to make us whole. God doesn't try to pretend that the loss has not taken place. He helps us find a new way of life as we adjust to the impact of the loss.

How are you changed and made whole again? God accomplishes this restoration through *spiritual intimacy*. This inside-out change is a benefit of the intimacy created through our relationship with God. And how is that done?

The apostle Paul gives us the basic steps to intimacy with God in his letter to the church at Philippi:

"Do not be anxious about anything, but in every situation, by prayer and petition, with thanksgiving, present your requests to God. And the peace of God, which transcends all understanding, will guard your hearts and your minds in Christ Jesus." (Philippians 4:6–7)

Separation may be the way of the world, even when intimacy is present. Families split apart. Marriages end in divorce or death. Friendships drift away. Yet separation is not what God has in mind for our intimacy with him. Healing comes from knowing that God will never leave you. He has given you many promises that you will never be separated from him, including the words of Jesus: "Surely I am with you always, to the very end of the age" (Matthew 28:20).

Spiritual intimacy leads to healing and full health. Lean into God's arms and experience the love and grace that he has for you.

Talk Daily with God

God wants to spend time with you. Granted, he is all-knowing and all-seeing, so he is aware of everything about your life before you mention anything to him. But God's eagerness to spend time with you goes beyond you coming to him with a list of requests.

Prayer can be considered an ongoing dialogue with God, a continual conversation with him.

You can ask for wisdom and guidance amid all your struggles. You can share your feelings and fears or talk about your daily concerns. Everyone on earth could use divine direction and understanding in their daily lives—and this is especially true for those struggling through a tough issue. Prayer is a powerful source of insight and inspiration as you pursue healing.

Consider talking with God about these things:

- Strength to live a courageous life

- A thankful spirit, maintaining gratitude during good and bad times

- God's power to utilize the talents and passions he has given you

- Wisdom to consistently make choices that show respect for yourself and others

- Health and healing—asking God to guide you steadily toward strength and comfort in your body, mind, and soul

Listen Closely: God Is Speaking to You

To hear the voice of God, you need to focus on what is being said to you. There is a time to cry out to God, and there is a time to be quiet. Solomon tells us there is a time to be silent and a time to speak (see Ecclesiastes 3:7). Not surprisingly, silence comes before speaking.

Some people scoff at the idea that God speaks, but only because they've never heard an audible voice answer their prayers directly. Prayer is a *conversation*—two-way communication. The truth is, God speaks all the time, and we would have no trouble

hearing him if we'd only broaden our definition of speech. The psalmist wrote:

> The heavens declare the glory of God; the skies proclaim the work of his hands. Day after day they pour forth speech; night after night they reveal knowledge. They have no speech, they use no words; no sound is heard from them. Yet their voice goes out into all the earth, their words to the ends of the world. (Psalm 19:1–4)

As this psalm so eloquently describes, God certainly speaks through nature. That message is one of majesty and grandeur to be sure, but also of balance, beauty, and rebirth—qualities we can cling to in perilous times.

That's just the beginning. God's voice can also be heard in art and music, in stories that inspire us to be more and do better. He speaks in every act of kindness, no matter how small. God's part of the conversation is found in sacred Scriptures and in the words of wise people throughout time who've labored to bring light into the darkness of ignorance. God speaks in our dreams and in subtle moments of intuition.

But, like in every conversation, it's possible to not hear a word of it. Why? Because you're not listening. Until you choose to *believe* God will answer your questions and calm your fears, it's likely you'll frantically do all the talking and never make room for his reply. To avoid this mistake, slow down, set aside time to be quiet, and extend your awareness. Begin noticing the variety of ways God has shown love to the world. Look closely. He will be sure you find them!

Cultivate Contentment

Think back to a moment when you felt perfectly at peace. Perhaps it was on a beach at sunset. You watched the sun touch the horizon in a burst of color, and suddenly felt the world was exactly as it should be.

CONTENTMENT HAS NOTHING TO DO WITH WHAT YOU HAVE OR DON'T HAVE, WHERE YOU ARE, OR WHO YOU'RE WITH.

Maybe it happened during a romantic dinner when time stood still. The world was never more beautiful than in that instant.

Savvy marketers would like you to believe the magical ingredient was the beach or the restaurant. Their message, delivered in countless advertisements and commercials, is that to be happy you must *go* somewhere else, *buy* something else, *be* someone else.

At the other end of the spectrum are those who believe that poverty is the only path to happiness. They preach a gospel of austerity and lack.

The truth isn't in either of these viewpoints or any-where in between. *Contentment has nothing to do with what you have or don't have, where you are, or who you're with.* Proof lies in the fact that unhappy people are found on every rung of the economic ladder.

Your contentment is within you. Contentment allows you to become more aware of the goodness and beauty in this world. Contentment is yours when you train your heart and mind to dwell on the abundance in your life and not the absences, the surplus and not the scarcity.

You needn't wait around for cosmic tumblers to fall into place. You don't need to win the proverbial lotto jackpot of life. You don't need more of anything. You can choose the experience of well-being and contentment anytime you like.

Contentment without Conditions

Wise men and women know that happiness and wellness are the result of accepting the impossible, doing without the indispensable, and bearing the intolerable. Yet some of us allow our lack of contentment to overpower us so that we compromise our physical, mental, emotional, and spiritual health.

Wouldn't we all have a better chance of experiencing contentment if we didn't place so many conditions on it? We lose ourselves in the world of *if only* . . .

- "If only my husband had a better-paying job, then I'd be happy."

- "If only my teenager didn't have such a bad attitude, then I'd be happy."

- "If only my boss wasn't such a jerk, then I'd be happy."

The conditions we demand for happiness are often what keep us from being content. Unfortunately, life is simply not fair, nor will it ever be. Justice will not always be served; tragedy will strike the innocent; the actions of the cruel will go unpunished. You and I may not approve of this troubling arrangement, but that's the way life is.

It takes only a cursory reading of the book of Job to understand that the upright will feel the sharp end of the stick as often as the scoundrel. To accept this as part of your belief system is to embark on a journey to peace, acceptance, and contentment.

We do well to follow the example of the apostle Paul, who wrote:

> I have learned to be content whatever the circumstances. I know what it is to be in need, and I know what it is to have plenty. I have learned the secret of being content in any and every

situation, whether well fed or hungry, whether living in plenty or in want. I can do all this through him who gives me strength. (Philippians 4:11–13)

Those are words that will lead us toward health, wholeness, and healing.

Join Hands *with* Fellow Travelers

Listen today to popular music and count the number of songs you hear about loneliness and isolation versus songs about being happy. Let's face it—most current songs are not about contentment, happiness, and finding true love.

Why is that? It has to do with the fact that most of us can relate to a singer's feelings of anguish and isolation. When we hurt from loneliness, there are few more powerful emotions. It's a universal condition.

As little ones, we get wounded—perhaps by parents who don't give us what we need emotionally or, in the worst case, abandon or abuse us. Or maybe we are exposed to trauma. We develop patterns of relating to people based on self-protection, safety, and security. We tend to isolate, take care of ourselves, and be an "island unto ourselves." We become suspicious of other people and begin to withdraw from those around us.

If we don't find the healing we need, we will be "duped" by our brain into believing things like:

1. I will only trust people so far, but if I let them in all the way, they will hurt or betray me.

2. In order to feel better, I need to act out with my "drug of choice" (i.e., alcohol, shopping, eating, sex, pornography).

3. In order to survive (especially emotionally), I must take care of myself.

Left alone in our pain, no matter its origin, we are cut off from the healing touch that comes from our relationships. Several factors reinforce our belief that it's better for us to be alone with our pain:

- We think others won't understand what we're going through.

- We're distrustful of others because of what we've suffered.

- We're unwilling to forgive those who have added to our pain.

- We're so depleted that we think we have nothing to give to another person.

- Because of what's happened to us, we don't believe we deserve to be loved again.

In each of these beliefs, there is an *element* of truth. Yet it is only partial truth. So how do we separate what is true (real issues) from the lies we believe that hold us back? Put differently, how do we cut through the misbeliefs that might have formed in the fog of our trauma?

Living with deep pain can be an all-encompassing experience. The pain keeps drawing our focus back to itself. When we're inwardly focused, it's easy to believe that other people don't understand what we're going through. Our pain becomes a badge—a "C" for cancer, a "D" for divorce, an "L" for the loss of a loved one. The pain becomes our identity. So, as we look around at others who wear no such badge, we assume we have nothing in common. We feel abjectly alone.

Suffering is universal. Since many of us choose to suffer in private, we are often unaware of the paths to healing others have taken. If we looked deeper, we'd be amazed at the wealth of experience, help, and compassion that's available through others.

We need to be open and honest with each other about the pain in our lives. We need to be willing to ask. When asked, we need to be willing to share. We need to be willing to pray for one another. This is the connection that brings healing. When we stay in isolation, our chances of achieving wholeness are slim at best.

Finding safe people to trust can be difficult, especially if you are coming out of an unhealthy relationship or lifestyle. I encourage you to ask God to lead you to those whom you can trust with your pain. Within the folds of God-directed relationships, we can mend our broken hearts, exchange loneliness for companionship, and participate in the double blessing of helping others to heal and being healed ourselves.

God sends us precious companions on our journey to healing. We were not meant to be alone. God can send each of us to encourage, rebuke, motivate, help, and love another person. As you develop friendships in your life, give some thought to these things:

- Be approachable and express genuine interest in others.

- Be aware that you need wise and thoughtful friends in your life, and you can offer that gift to others.

- Be considerate and kind. Everyone wants a friend who models those behaviors.

- Be prayerful and ask God to lead you to people with whom you can develop solid and positive friendships.

Find this type of friend for yourself. Be this type of friend to others.

Believe *That* God Leads *and* Guides

At the heart of maintaining stability and balance must be this unshakable belief: God is in control—in your life and in the world. After our best-laid plans have been organized and implemented, God is in control.

When we do our homework, pay our dues, and sit back to wait for things to go our way, God is still in control.

As I consider closing thoughts for you, my mind travels back in time. In 1989, my wife, LaFon, and I decided to set out and launch a counseling clinic. I had finished my doctoral studies just a few years before, and LaFon and I were early in our marriage. We encountered all the challenges and struggles of a couple building a life together and pursuing careers.

Many people considered the opening of a clinic to be a foolish attempt that would go nowhere. For us, however, it was an act of faith as we began the counseling practice with only one room. Nothing but four walls, with no waiting room, no receptionist, no amenities . . . and not many clients, either. We were just two young people with a dream to reach out to individuals and families

> ## God Isn't Finished with You Yet
>
> "BEING CONFIDENT OF THIS, THAT HE WHO BEGAN A GOOD WORK IN YOU WILL CARRY IT ON TO COMPLETION UNTIL THE DAY OF CHRIST JESUS." (PHILIPPIANS 1:6)
>
> "FOR WE ARE GOD'S HANDIWORK, CREATED IN CHRIST JESUS TO DO GOOD WORKS, WHICH GOD PREPARED IN ADVANCE FOR US TO DO." (EPHESIANS 2:10)

struggling to work through problems and find peace in turbulent times.

I wonder if we would have taken so many risks had we known what it takes to make dreams come true. If we had foreseen the painful days of burnout and emotional exhaustion, the months when many clients chose not to pay their bills, the times when we would look at each other and wonder aloud if it was worth the effort.

GOD CARES DEEPLY FOR YOU, YOUR PLANS, AND YOUR DREAMS.

But through it all, we believed in our hearts that God gave us this dream and he was in control. We knew he would rule in our successes and our failures—and he did. Today we can say that he was with us in times of trouble and times of tranquility, times of privation and times of plenty. He was with us during our moments of courage and during our moments of doubt.

All these years later, the tiny counseling practice we started has grown into The Center: A Place of Healing, serving many clients each year with an excellent staff of medical experts and support staff. I tell you this to show that God truly does lead, guide, and direct our lives. Only through his power and grace have I achieved many of my professional and personal dreams . . . and I am profoundly thankful to him.

As you continue your journey toward health and healing, believe with your whole heart that God cares deeply for you, your plans, and your dreams. He is holding you firmly and tenderly in his mighty hands.

Notes

Key #1

1. "Positive Thinking: Stop Negative Self-Talk to Reduce Stress," Mayo Clinic, February 18, 2017, https://www .mayoclinic.org/healthy-lifestyle/stress-management /in-depth/positive-thinking/art-20043950.

2. Les Parrott, *Love the Life You Live* (Wheaton, IL: Tyndale, 2003), 27, 29.

Key #2

3. Gareth Cook, "Why We Are Wired to Connect," *Scientific American*, October 13, 2013, https://www .scientificamerican.com/article/why-we-are-wired -to-connect.

Key #3

1. Neil Clark Warren, *Catching the Rhythm of Love* (Nashville, TN: Thomas Nelson, 2000), 18.

Key #4

1. "Communications Technology in the Bedroom," Sleep in America Poll, National Sleep Foundation, https://sleepfoundation.org/sites/default/files /sleepinamericapoll/SIAP_2011_Summary_of _Findings.pdf.

2. Samuel Harvey et al, "Exercise and the Prevention of Depression," American Journal of Psychiatry 175, no. 1 (October 3, 2017), https://ajp.psychiatryonline.org /action/doSearch?AllField=depression+exercise.

3. "Regular Physical Activity Can Produce Long-term Health Benefits," Office of Disease Prevention and Health Promotion, 2008, https://health.gov /paguidelines/guidelines/summary.aspx.

4. "How Much Physical Activity Do Adults Need?" Centers of Disease Control and Prevention, 2018, https://www.cdc.gov/physicalactivity/basics/adults /index.htm.

5. Marily Oppezzo et al, "Give Your Ideas Some Legs: The Positive Effect of Walking on Creative Thinking," Journal of Experimental Psychology 40, no. 4 (2014): 1142–52, http://psycnet.apa.org/record/2014-14435 -001.

MORE RESOURCES FROM
DR. GREGORY L. JANTZ

**Unmasking Emotional Abuse:
Start the Healing**
ISBN: 9781628623765

Six Steps to Reduce Stress
ISBN: 9781628623673

**Ten Tips for Parenting
the Smartphone Generation**
ISBN: 9781628623703

**Five Keys to Dealing
with Depression**
ISBN: 9781628623611

**Five Keys to Health and
Healing: Hope for Body,
Mind, and Spirit**
ISBN: 9781628628203

Seven Answers for Anxiety
ISBN: 9781628623642

Five Keys to Raising Boys
ISBN: 9781628623734

**40 Answers for
Teens' Top Questions**
ISBN: 9781628624236

www.hendricksonrose.com